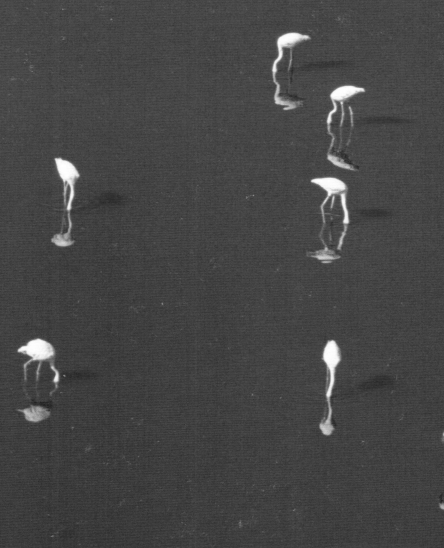

Untamed

Animals Around the World

Library of Congress Cataloging-in-Publication Data has been applied for.
ISBN 0-8109-5956-9

Copyright © 2005, Éditions de La Martinière Jeunesse, France
2, rue Christine – 75006 Paris
English translation copyright © 2005 Harry N. Abrams, Inc.

Photographs copyright © 2005 Steve Bloom
www.stevebloom.com

Designed by Jay Colvin

Published in 2005 by Harry N. Abrams, Incorporated, New York.
All rights reserved. No part of the contents of this book may be reproduced without the written permission of the publisher.

Printed and bound in Belgium
10 9 8 7 6 5 4 3 2 1

Harry N. Abrams, Inc.
100 Fifth Avenue
New York, NY 10011
www.abramsbooks.com

Abrams is a subsidiary of

LA MARTINIÈRE

Untamed
Animals Around the World

Photographs by Steve Bloom

Text by
Christian Havard

Illustrations by
Emmanuelle Zicot

HARRY N. ABRAMS, INC., PUBLISHERS

CONTENTS

Getting Around

Rivalry

Courtship

Animals and Their Young

Play

In the Water

Sleeping

Feeding

The Rhythm of the Seasons

Life in Extreme Conditions

Endangered Species

Photographing the Animal World

Some time ago, Steve Bloom took a safari in South Africa, and, like any other tourist, he took his camera along. This trip, however, was not just a quick getaway from the grind of daily life. In fact, it changed his life. On his return to England, Steve decided to become a wildlife photographer. However, as he discovered while watching the behavior of a gorilla in a zoo, Steve was not just interested in photographing animals, but also in what sort of life these animals led in the wild. So he began to travel around the globe to observe, and photograph, animals in their natural environments.

After two years primarily photographing primates like the gorilla, orangutan, and chimpanzee, Steve began to take an interest in other animals. Although he travels to many countries, Africa is the place he loves most—hardly surprising, since this is where he was born and raised.

What is most astonishing about Steve's photographs is that they seem to have been taken from just feet away—you feel you could almost touch the animals. But for safety, Steve only approaches animals that are used to meeting human beings. To photograph the more dangerous creatures, he uses a camera with high-powered telescopic lenses. Every situation, however, is unique, and he constantly has to adapt: He photographs lions from his car, using it as a shield. When approaching grizzly bears in Alaska—they hate being surprised—he talks loudly and continuously to warn them he's coming; if he tried to creep up on them, the bears might react violently and attack. But in spite of all these precautions, Steve has been in

some seriously scary situations. Once, in India, he was perched on the back of a vehicle photographing rhinos when one of them suddenly charged. There was no time to take evasive action but, fortunately, the animal changed course at the last moment and Steve and his team escaped unharmed.

A quality essential to any photographer's art is patience. Steve once decided, against all odds, to try to capture on camera a great white shark leaping out of the water. He spent more than fifteen days on a small boat, his eye glued to the camera's viewfinder, roasting in the fierce sun, and with his stomach churning from seasickness before he finally got his chance. Even under such arduous conditions, Steve managed to catch this magnificent spectacle—a spectacle lasting only a second or two.

Many animals are particularly dear to Steve Bloom: endangered species, such as pandas and Siberian tigers. Because so very few remain in the wild, it's a rare event indeed to photograph them there. So Steve also photographs them in wildlife parks in China that reproduce these creatures' natural environment, protecting them and preventing their total disappearance.

Photographing wildlife is a wonderful way to make a living, a privilege in fact, with each day bringing a new crop of surprises. But over and above Steve's passion for photography and animals is the challenge of making the whole world aware of just how close so many species are to extinction.

On Foot and in the Air

In the forests of Madagascar, Verreaux's sifaka, the creature on the left with its young, sometimes travels on its hind legs. The leopard shown below is preparing to leap into a tree in search of prey.

Animals travel around—whether on foot or by air—to hunt for food, migrate to adjust to the changing seasons, escape enemies, establish a new nest, or win new territory.

The world of animals is wonderfully complex—a universal ballet with a cast of creatures endlessly running, soaring, fleeing, whirling, skating, and swimming. If they stop moving, it's to watch for prey—like the leopard lying in ambush—or to hide from a predator, rest, bask in the sun, protect themselves from the cold and wind, or sleep. They also stop moving around in order to give birth or hatch their eggs—to bring forth new life, like this baby Verreaux's sifaka clinging to its mother's back.

All land mammals walk on four feet, and hence are called quadrupeds. The only exception is humans, who are bipeds. When they leave the trees to travel on the ground, some of the larger apes (the gorilla and chimpanzee) and lemurs (the sifaka and ringtail) also walk upright.

Most birds fly, but some are flightless (ratites), such as the ostrich and the rhea.

The okapi, a Congolese cousin of the giraffe, walks by raising both feet on one side of its body at the same time. This type of gait is known as "ambling."

Speed and Endurance

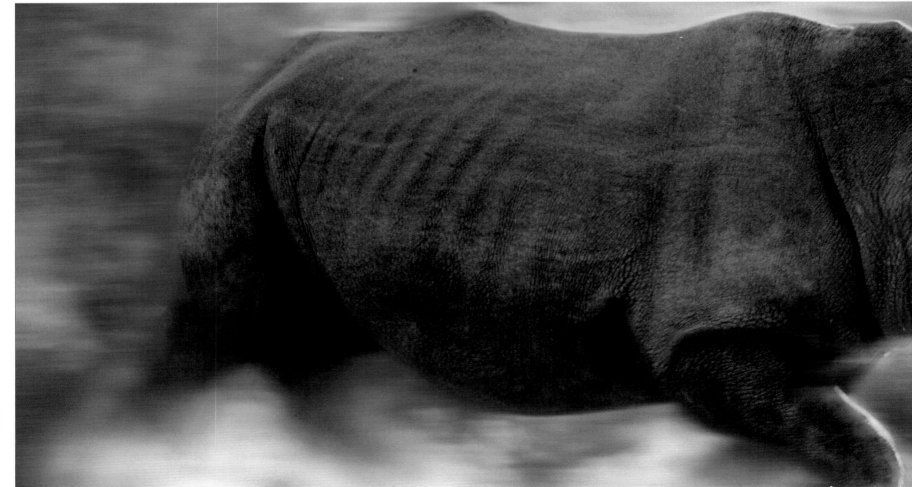

The cheetah is the fastest of the cats. Over a short distance (a few dozen yards or so), it can reach 70 miles per hour. The white rhinoceros is somewhat less agile—after all, it has one and a half to three tons of bulk to move around! But it can still manage to run almost 30 miles per hour.

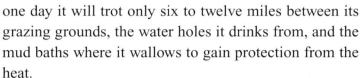

The white rhinoceros seldom travels very far. In one day it will trot only six to twelve miles between its grazing grounds, the water holes it drinks from, and the mud baths where it wallows to gain protection from the heat.

The cheetah, too, doesn't move around much since there is usually prey in its immediate vicinity. On the other hand, catching it is never easy. Even if it gets as close as possible to its victims, they can run fast as well. For example, the impala can do 45 miles per house, with bounds 32 feet long and 10 feet high! Eight times out of ten, it escapes. The cheetah is, in fact, a sprinter: it runs fast but is soon exhausted. It then takes a long time to recover.

The animal world also has its marathoners, those animals that can travel great distances: the elephant, the wolf, the reindeer. The reason they wander, however, is always the same: the search for food.

Elephants live in herds and their appetites are enormous: they each eat between 300 and 500 pounds of grass and leaves a day, depending on the season. If the herd were to stay in the same place, it would quickly consume all available food. So it travels hundreds of miles, always taking the same route, before returning to its point of departure . . . and then setting off again. These migrations result in careful conservation of resources, since vegetation is able to regrow during the herd's absences.

The wolf can run for long distances without tiring. It can trot at about 12 miles per hour, with top speeds of 30 miles per hour in deep snow in the wide open spaces of Canada.

In the Water

The Camargue is the realm of bulls, birds, horses . . . and water. These magnificent, semi-wild members of the horse family run freely among its salt marshes and countless streams.

At birth, the Camargue foal is completely black. As it grows, it turns gray, and, on reaching adulthood, it acquires a white coat. Water is these horses' playground, but they share it with the region's bulls and a huge variety of birds: the little egret, the pink flamingo, and the marsh harrier, for instance. And if the water in a channel is too deep to wade, it doesn't matter: these horses are excellent swimmers and nothing can stand in the way of their freedom.

Most mammals can swim naturally, with the exception of some great apes. The orangutan, for instance, sometimes visits a pond or a stream to nibble a few aquatic plants, but it merely stands in the water, close to the bank, sometimes hanging onto a branch with one hand.

Some animals are totally dependent on the aquatic environment. The hippopotamus (actually a cousin of the horse) spends the whole day in the water to protect its delicate skin from the African sun. It rests and swims and even walks on the lakebed—not at all bothered by its one and a half to two and a half ton weight. It's in the water that the big males challenge each other for the favor of the females. They also reproduce in the water. They wait for the sun to go down before clambering onto the land to graze the grass.

The Camargue is also a paradise for the pink flamingo. This bird uses its curious curved beak to filter small shellfish, larvae, and algae from the water.

Animal Acrobats

Leaping from branch to branch is the preferred mode of travel for most monkeys—as well as their favorite game. In the Borneo jungle, a mother proboscis monkey, her baby clinging to her belly, launches herself into the air to reach another tree.

The conquest of the skies—this is the wonderful heritage of birds. They are the only creatures with wings and so we think of them as the only ones that fly. But in fact, birds have to share the kingdom of the air with a few very special mammals.

The best known of these mammals, and the true "fliers" of the bunch, are the bats. The membrane that connects the long fingers on their hands, their hind legs, and their tails serves as a wing. Most bats are nocturnal and therefore specialists in night flying. They swirl around chasing after insects using an ultrasound system known as "echolocation": on encountering a target, the sound wave created by their cries bounces back to them as an echo.

Other mammals, such as flying squirrels, are actually gliders. The skin stretched between their legs and bellies (the patagium) enables them to travel several yards in the air, from tree to tree.

As for the monkeys, most are acrobats of the high treetops. Thanks to their hands and tails, they can latch on to the smallest branch to perform their aerial gymnastics. Watch them carefully—they are true performers! Every leap is calculated—there's no question of missing the intended branch, as a fall could be fatal. Moving around like this is also a way of avoiding having to climb down to the ground, where they could expose themselves to predators.

The Antarctic cold and storms hold no terror for the wandering albatross. With its nine-foot wing span, it often takes advantage of air currents to glide, and rest its wings.

Private Property!

The bald eagle is an ace acrobat. Looping the loop, flying on its back, pirouetting—the eagle executes the most complicated maneuvers to make life difficult for rivals.

In the animal kingdom, very little is done on a whim; rather, everything is based on instinct—eating (and avoiding being eaten), sleeping, and the perpetuation of the species. To achieve these three objectives, animals must first find the most suitable habitat, a space they can conquer and defend—what we call their territory.

Perched on a big tree close to its nest during the breeding season, the bald eagle keeps watch over its territory. It will defend it by force if necessary against any other eagle that tries to take it. No trespassers are permitted—the female is sitting on her eggs and mustn't be disturbed. Nor can other eagles nest too close. If they did, there wouldn't be enough prey to go around once the young are born. If a fight breaks out, screams and threatening flight maneuvers are usually enough to frighten off interlopers.

Animals that live on the ground behave in much the same way, but frequently they also mark their territory. Thus wolves in a pack regularly patrol the perimeter of their territory, leaving droppings or spraying the ground with urine. Other packs are thus warned to keep their distance. If any pack ignores this boundary and hunts in the other's area, a battle will ensue. There aren't many violent clashes however, and the weaker animals will soon give way to the stronger.

In a herring gull colony, territory is divided very simply. It's just a matter of keeping out of reach of your neighbor's beak when you're sitting on your nest.

Dominance and Social Status

Beware of boxing kangaroos! Actually, kangaroos don't box—this is just a myth created by humans. In the violent fighting between gray kangaroos seen below, the terrific blows these animals inflict on their opponents' stomachs are produced with the hind legs.

Among polygamous species, the male must gather as many females to himself as possible. He must then hang onto them by forming a harem which he watches over and protects from his rivals.

In the semi-desert plains of the Australian outback, gray kangaroos live in small family groups, or "mobs," consisting of one male, two or three females, and the three or four youngest offspring. The females are very fertile and capable of taking care of up to three differently aged young simultaneously: a baby at a nipple, a joey in the mother's pouch, and a bigger one at her side. The young males are always ready to take the place of the dominant males, and there are frequent confrontations. In spite of their powerful kick, these kangaroos' fights are never fatal and end as soon as one animal realizes he is the weaker opponent and retreats.

The outback is also the domain of the dingo, a small wild dog (between 35 and 45 pounds in weight and 15 to 20 inches tall) which lives in a dispersed pack. This pack comprises several families and some lone animals. They all defend the territory, and big prey (such as gray and red kangaroos) are hunted by the whole pack. Young males and females regularly leave the pack to join other groups. This prevents interbreeding and introduces fresh blood to the various families.

The Australian desert is the last place in the world where flocks of wild dromedaries can be found. Sadly, even here their numbers are declining.

Peaceful Conquest

The red-crowned crane, known in Japan as the "Goddess of the Marshes," was designated an "outstanding natural monument" by the Japanese authorities in 1952. At that time there were only about thirty left. The species is now fully protected and, today their numbers have increased to around a thousand.

Red-crowned cranes gather on the marshes in winter to perform their courtship rituals. In pairs, beaks gaping and wings spread, the male and female birds dance with leaps, bows, and rhythmic steps. They toss grass and twigs into the air while emitting loud, trumpet-like cries. Once mated, a pair bonds for life. And they continue to dance for each other all year round.

Another great performer of the animal world is the western capercaillie, which lives in the massif of the Vosges. Year after year, the males gather to dance in the same place. Solemnly singing, plumage ashimmer, and throats swelling, they squabble with flapping wings as they confront each other under the apparently indifferent gaze of the females. Yet those bored hens will choose the lucky victor when the display is over. The cock, however, is pretty fickle. After mating with the first hen, he'll come back and dance again, hoping to make another conquest.

Some birds even offer their partners a present to seduce them—a pebble or a twig for the nest. To show off his hunting skills, the cormorant presents his chosen mate with a gift of a fish.

His tail spread like a fan and beak raised, the blue-footed booby dances by lifting his big, webbed feet as high as he can.

Conquest by Force

The tiger will not tolerate any other males on his territory—only females. So when a rival crosses his border, a fight is inevitable; there isn't space enough for the two of them.

In the wild, it's common for males to fight over females. These confrontations are ritualized: threatening postures, possibly a fight, followed by the retreat of the weaker male. The death of one of the combatants is rare, and always the result of an accident. A deep scratch may, for example, result in an infection and hence the death of a tiger. Similarly, two stags may get their antlers entangled and die of starvation, unable to extricate themselves. Walrus battles have a reputation for ferocity—a male may be ripped open by a tusk and succumb to his injuries.

The orangutan's behavior is not exactly gentlemanly. A male doesn't fight with males, but females. If a female ventures onto his territory, he forces her to mate with him in order to pass on his own genes.

But the fiercest creature in terms of winning a mate is the bird chosen as a symbol of peace: the dove. Sometimes the stronger male will pursue his adversary as he flies away after a fight; if he catches him, he'll beat him to death!

The female praying mantis has the charming habit of devouring the male after mating. She performs this cannibalistic act because she needs an immediate source of protein if her body is to manufacture eggs.

Who's the Lucky One?

The scarlet macaw (or Ara macao) originated in South America. It lives in family groups in forests of very tall, sparse trees. Like all parrots, however, it is under threat from the trade in tropical birds.

In the bird kingdom, it's the female who chooses her partner. The lucky male will be the one with the handsomest plumage or the finest song, or who can make the coziest nest. All these qualities are signs that a creature's in good health and therefore most likely to produce robust offspring.

All scarlet macaws have identically colored plumage. So when choosing her mate, the female will base her decision on the quality and length of the male's feathers and his cries. Hard luck, therefore, on anyone who's spoiled his feathers, got parasites or lost his voice—he doesn't have a chance! The couples that result are very closely bonded, and pair for life.

The male peacock is a regular Casanova. He has 150 long, highly developed back feathers, often incorrectly thought to be tail feathers. To draw attention to himself, he extends these feathers like a fan and sets them quivering. He folds his wings, lifts his tail and struts around the females. The females watch this display and then choose the best looking male. Sometimes a small group of females will form around a male, waiting while he mates several times with each of them.

This female hamadryas baboon is displaying her scarlet rump to show she's ready to mate.

Family Life

Lions live in family groups, called prides, composed of lionesses, their cubs, and one or two dominant males. After three and a half months of gestation, the lioness produces three or four young. She lives alone with her cubs for a few weeks before rejoining the pride.

Communal life has certain advantages. In a pride of lions and lionesses, all the cubs are born at the same time. When they get together, the whole group takes care of the cubs. The females help one another, benefiting from each other's experience. Sometimes a cub will even take milk from someone else's mother! In addition, group life gives cubs little opportunity to be naughty, since there's always an adult to keep an eye on them. But the cubs face a much greater great risk: if the pride's dominant male is replaced by another male, he will kill them all to safeguard his own bloodline. Females deprived of their young in this way will immediately come into heat, ready to produce more cubs.

Far from the African savanna, on the high plateaus of the Andes, the vicuna (a cousin of the llama) brings just one kid into the harem. As soon as it's born it tries to stand up. After half an hour or so of repeated struggles and falls, it finally staggers to the comfort of its mother. An hour later it's galloping and cavorting around her. Like the lion cubs, the baby is made welcome by all the mothers, and it quickly joins in exploring and playing with other young herd members.

The wild rabbit may have from one to seven litters of between three and twelve young a year—which makes an average of four litters of five young a year, or twenty babies!

Single Mothers

Springtime. In a flooded meadow, bear cubs trot after their mother. She's anxious to reach cover—even for powerful animals like these, walking in the open is always dangerous, and even more caution is essential with young around.

A mother's life is not an easy one: most males leave their partners after mating, and the females must bring up their young and protect them on their own. The female bear gives birth to one to three cubs in a well-concealed den—often a cave with an entrance screened by bushes. The little bear cub weighs scarcely a full pound at birth, its eyes are closed, and it's virtually hairless. It will stay in the den with its mother for almost four months before venturing outside. Although weaned at 18 months, it won't be independent until it's two or three years old. When accompanied by her young, the female is careful to avoid meeting males because their reactions are unpredictable and they may attack small cubs.

But not all fathers are like the bear. The coyote, which lives on the plains of North America, is a model father. When the arrival of his offspring is imminent, he hunts alone to bring the female food as she waits to give birth in the burrow they've chosen together. When the babies are born, he helps groom them with energetic licking. He guards the entrance to the den and keeps intruders out. When the young begin to eat meat, he brings them their first prey and, later, teaches them how to hunt for themselves.

Beaks agape, these robin chicks await their next mouthful. Their parents take turns feeding them all day long.

Bringing Up Baby

A mother orangutan full of tenderness and affection for her baby. She suckles it for three to four years before contemplating a new birth. If all goes well, she'll have an average of five babies during her lifetime.

Bringing up the young is the work of either the mother alone or both parents. Once the young have grown up, they are often forcibly ejected from the family home by their parents, who are preparing for new births. The youngsters must then fend for themselves, with no hope of ever rejoining their family.

A mother orangutan looks after her baby by herself, and it's by watching its mother that the youngster learns. Very quickly the mother teaches her baby how to swing on a vine, how to walk, and how to leap among the trees. She shows it how to distinguish leaves and fruit that are good to eat from those that are poisonous. By protecting herself, the mother instructs her baby about the dangers of its environment: predators, for instance, or dangerous actions like uncontrolled leaps. And when the time comes for them to part, with the youngster some five or six years old, she will drive it out . . . for good.

The female cuckoo is the most ruthless of creatures: she forces a couple of strangers to foster her child. She has the nasty habit of laying her eggs in the nest of another bird, such as a dunnock or warbler. When the baby cuckoo hatches, it immediately tosses the other eggs out of the nest—even the other chicks if they were hatched first! Once it's the only bird in the nest, its adoptive parents will have to keep on feeding it, even if it turns out to be five times their size!

A young Eleonora's falcon hesitates before launching itself into the void. After 40 days in the nest, the great moment has arrived for its first flight.

Protecting the Little Ones

When in a hurry, a lioness will pick up her young cub by the scruff, carrying it unharmed in her mouth. The female elephant always keeps one eye on her calf to ensure it is close by her side.

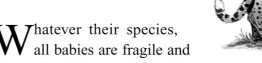

Whatever their species, all babies are fragile and vulnerable. There's always a predator waiting to take advantage of a moment's distraction on the part of the parents and carry off and devour a young one. So every kind of animal has developed strategies to protect its offspring as best it can.

Elephant calves faced with danger take refuge between the legs of adults. On the icy tundra of the Arctic, young musk oxen do the same when the white wolf attacks. But the wolf has his work cut out: as soon a wolf pack is spotted, the musk oxen form a circle, with their heads facing outward. The young then take refuge behind the adults, where they'll be safe. The wolves find themselves confronted by a solid barrier of huge, pointed horns; only by force of numbers and cunning do they sometimes manage to break through and carry off a young calf.

When their mother goes off hunting, young leopards are also in danger. Still too small to accompany her, they hide in thickets or holes. But hyenas are always on the prowl and sometimes find their hiding places. Hyenas show no mercy; they carry the young leopards off and eat them. One of the mother leopard's tricks is to move her young regularly, carrying them in her mouth from one hiding place to another.

These fox cubs are playing in the grass under their mother's watchful eye. At the slightest sign of danger, the whole family runs and hides in the den.

Lessons for Life

This young grizzly bear is trying to catch gulls as they swoop over the riverbank. He is still learning hunting skills.

Young animals play to test their abilities, establish a pecking order, and learn the lessons of life.

A young deer fawn joins the herd of does with its mother one or two weeks after birth. There it meets other young deer. Playing allows them to hone their skills as they chase after each other, cavorting over the meadows. The bigger they grow, the farther away from the females their games take them. This way they gradually distance themselves from their mothers and learn to be independent.

Through play, especially mock fights, young bear cubs learn who's the strongest or bravest. When they climb trees, there's always one who goes higher than all the rest or ventures out along the thinnest branch. Playing improves agility and, above all, teaches young how to assess risks—the cubs must learn not to fall.

It may seem like a cruel game to us when cats play with their prey before eating it. Lynx cubs, for instance, do this when their parents bring them a live field mouse. The youngsters amuse themselves letting it go and catching it time and again; they prod it and bat it around with their paws before turning it into a meal. In fact, it's the way cubs practice their hunting skills.

Lion cubs use the adults as their playground, grabbing their tail tufts, pulling their ears, and climbing on Daddy's back—the fun is endless!

Adults Play, Too

Sheltered in her lair and after a hibernation lasting several months, the mother polar bear gives birth in January to two cubs. The babies divide their time between playing and resting.

It's not only young animals who play. Adults do, too, with their young or among themselves, for the sheer pleasure of it.

Even though polar bears live alone (the male on his own and the female with her young), encounters do take place on the ice floes. After the customary formalities establishing dominance—who has to give way to whom—the bears take a short break to relax. Then the mock fights begin, the dance routines that briefly enliven the vast white desert. When all is over, each bear goes its own way again.

The wolf is a bit of a joker: it hides behind a rock or a bush and waits for another member of the pack to pass by, then jumps out at it. A battle follows, but a friendly one, which the two wolves thoroughly enjoy. Indeed, they're often joined by other pack members, and the scuffle turns into one great big, happy, free for all.

And then there are the crows, an impressive sight swirling, pirouetting, and diving. They wheel through the air on their backs, singly or in groups, cawing raucously. Some have even been spotted "skating" on frozen lakes or down the slopes of snow-covered roofs.

The otter uses the riverbanks like a water slide. It slips through the water on its back or tummy, then climbs up the bank and starts all over again!

Marine Mammals

The bottlenose dolphin lives in groups called schools in tropical and temperate seas. This excellent swimmer can reach speeds of 30 miles per hour—no mean feat for a giant measuring up to 13 feet in length and with a maximum weight of over a thousand pounds!

Contrary to what some people think, whales, seals, and dolphins are not fish: they are marine mammals. Hence they have to surface regularly to breathe (they have lungs, not gills) and, like all mammals, they suckle their young.

At low tide in the Somme Estuary in France, you'll often see groups of twenty or so young seal cubs stretched out on the sand banks, asleep. When the tide rises and tickles their tummies, they swim out to sea to hunt. They consume only four to six pounds of crustaceans and small fish a day, despite their body weight of between 100 and 250 pounds.

Baby seals are born at the beginning of July. On the sand, the pup, or baby seal, sucks at one of its mother's two teats for about one minute out of every four hours for three to five months. From birth, it can stay underwater for two minutes, then later for up to ten, before it needs to surface for air.

Unlike the seal, the dolphin gives birth and suckles her young—for one year—in the water. Her two teats are located at the base of her belly. An adult dolphin can remain submerged without breathing for some eight minutes, diving to a depth of over 800 feet.

With its horse's head, fat belly, and lizardlike tail, the seahorse must be one of the strangest looking fish!

Deep Sea Sailors

The humpback whale is a member of the Cetacean family. Instead of teeth, it has "baleens," or bony combs, which filter the sea water for krill (plankton and small shellfish), its staple diet.

Most marine mammals are great travelers. In summer, the humpback is usually found in the cold northern seas from Norway to Newfoundland. In winter it returns to the warm waters of Central and South America to breed off Hawaii, in the Caribbean, and around the Marianas. It's at this time that the whales' song is most likely to be heard. It can resemble the bellowing of a stag, an opera aria, or even a nightingale's serenade. Lasting some ten to thirty minutes, it's audible several miles away.

On its long voyages, the whale maintains a cruising speed of two to four miles per hour. However, when hunting or if it—or its calf—is attacked, it can reach almost 15 miles per hour!

In spite of its 30 tons, the whale is extremely agile, playful, and a great show-off. It can rear up vertically to look around (this is called "spy hopping"), leap out of the water ("breaching"), sometimes shaking its fins, and can lash the water violently with its tail, splashing all and sundry!

Like the baleen whale, the sperm whale and the narwhal travel the oceans from north to south, but their route remains a mystery.

Forget the mythical unicorn: its horn is nothing more than the male narwhal's upper left canine, which can grow to eight feet long!

Sharing the Oceans

In the cold seas of the Antarctic, Adélie penguins enjoy an extraordinary playground. In groups called packs, they jump, climb and slide on the ice floes before diving into the water.

Fish and marine mammals share the world's waters with other animals: reptiles (such as turtles), birds (such as penguins), and even mammals that are primarily land-dwellers (such as otters).

The leatherback is the biggest of the turtle family, measuring up to six feet in length and weighing an average of almost 900 pounds. With its front legs outspread, it spans nine feet! A solitary creature, the leatherback tirelessly journeys thousands of miles across the world's seas. The female returns to land every two years, where she lays a hundred or so eggs in a single night.

The Adélie penguin lives in the Antarctic. Every year it returns to the same beach to lay its eggs and raise its two chicks, which struggle to be served first when the adults bring home a fish dinner. When small, they feed on krill that their parents regurgitate. From their twentieth day, they are gathered in huge nurseries of several thousand chicks. As they grow, they begin to eat fish and small squid.

The sea otter prefers the sunny coasts of California. Although a land mammal, it spends its whole life in water, most of the time just floating on its back. It eats, gives birth, and sleeps in the water (it sleeps rolled up in weeds so the current doesn't carry it away).

The killer whale is a formidable hunter. It takes advantage of big waves to hurl itself onto the beach and snatch a sea lion.

Hibernation, Aestivation, and Extended Sleep

Large male polar bears don't hibernate. They simply lie down on the snow-covered ice and nap, protected by their thick fur and almost four inches of fat beneath their skin.

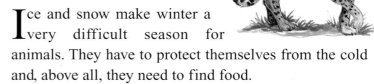

Ice and snow make winter a very difficult season for animals. They have to protect themselves from the cold and, above all, they need to find food.

Some animals, such as the dormouse and the marmot, choose to hibernate. They spend the month of September gorging themselves on grains, grass, and fruit, accumulating as much fat as possible. Then, sheltered safely in nests or burrows, they sleep deeply and continuously from October to April. Their heart rhythm slows down and their breathing drops to almost 1 percent of its normal rate. They wake up very thin, but ready for the return of spring.

Other animals have a different way of beating cold and hunger. To reduce the amount of energy they use, and hence their food requirements, they simply sleep for longer each day, keeping all activity to a minimum.

The polar bear, for example, hollows out a kind of igloo in a snowdrift, while the red squirrel insulates his drey with moss and dry grass. Though they all settle down to sleep as long as possible, they have regular waking periods to stretch their legs and perhaps eat and drink. These waking times may be hard on the squirrel's memory—will it be able to find all the caches of seeds and nuts it created before going to sleep?

In summer, to protect themselves from the searing heat, many amphibians and snails cease all activity and sink into a prolonged sleep. This is called "aestivation."

Sleep Patterns

Where could be a nicer place for a nap than a sandy beach? The elephant seal rests for much of the day, between excursions into the water to look for food and occasional attempts to meet a mate.

All animals sleep, whether alone or in groups: this is an important function of life. But time of day in which they sleep vary between species. Some are "diurnal," meaning they sleep at night, while others are "nocturnal," resting during the day.

On the beach, the elephant seal is safe—there are no other animals to threaten it, so it can rest all day and night without fear. It doesn't even need to make a nest, being quite happy to sleep on the bare ground. But this is not the case for all animals.

Every evening, the chimpanzee builds itself a shelter of branches and leaves in a tree. The young are excused this chore and allowed to share their mother's bed. Like humans, the great apes sleep about eight hours a night.

Sleep patterns are often influenced by an animal's predators. Whereas herbivores (such as the zebra, gnu, and Thomson's gazelle) sleep about three hours a night—mostly on their feet so they can flee at the first sign of danger—lions and leopards can afford up to 10 hours' rest, settled comfortably and safely in the shade.

There are some animals with really weird sleeping habits. For example, in the tundra, the swan spends the night huddled under the snow. More surprising, perhaps, the swift sleeps only a few minutes a day—while flying! The bat, on the other hand, rests hanging upside down from a beam or the walls and roofs of caves.

The sloth (also known as the ai or unau) must surely owe its name to the twenty hours it sleeps every day!

Fair Shares?

When the great white shark is hunting fish, it sometimes encounters a sea lion. Will the sea lion manage to escape the jaws of this huge beast?

Animals frequently share a meal, but not always by design. When a shark has caught its prey, for example, its companions will gather around it in hopes getting a portion of feast. There won't be a fight: there's just enough for the strongest and smartest. No shark intentionally shares its food; if it can wolf down its catch in one go without leaving anything for the others, it will certainly do so!

On the African savanna, there's a strict pecking order at mealtimes. Regardless of which animal caught the prey, each one receives its share of food in turn, starting with the strongest.

So when a lioness catches a gnu, it's the males in the pride who help themselves first. The lioness and her cubs must wait. The hyenas will then wait until the lions have finished to snatch a few morsels. Next come the jackals—they make do with what the hyenas have left. That's not the end of it, though: it's the vultures' turn to tear off the last shreds of skin. One of them, the lammergeier or bearded vulture, even flies away with the bones—it then drops them to the ground, breaking them open to reveal the marrow.

Finally, once the insects have had their share, all traces of the carcass will have disappeared.

The great frigate bird has devised an ingenious method of feeding: it steals the fish from other birds in midflight.

Hunting Techniques

With an expert swipe of its great paw, a grizzly bear catches a salmon in midair. When the bears are fishing, the best spots will be occupied by the dominant and older of the species.

Animals adopt various techniques for getting a meal, depending on the intended prey: ambushes, surprise attacks, chases, beating through the undergrowth, looting, etc.

Pelicans have a very peculiar way of fishing. Ten or so get together in shallow water, where they swim in a tight semi-circle. When they spot a shoal of fish, they all simultaneously plunge their beaks into the water and withdraw them. The pouches under their beaks (the gular pouch) serve as nets! They swallow their share of the catch, and the ballet-like routine starts all over again. The pelican chicks will now be able to thrust their heads into their parents' bills to eat regurgitated pap (soft food) and small fish.

The brown bear is a loner who can adapt to any culinary situation; it eats whatever it finds on its wanderings. After fishing, it delicately picks a fruit or a berry before savoring it. Sometimes it will scratch at the ground, expose a nest of field mice, and eat the entire family. If it finds a hive, it licks out the honey with no fear of being stung by the angry bees, protected as it is by its long, thick coat. And if hunger leads a brown bear to a sheepfold, it will break down the gate and carry off a ewe or a lamb.

The anteater, as its name suggests, feeds solely on ants. It catches them with its narrow, sticky tongue, which is almost 25 inches long!

Win Some, Lose Some!

The Adélie penguin, like the king penguin, feeds mainly on fish and small squid. In the breeding season, the males and females take turns sitting on the eggs and, once they are hatched, bring food to the chicks.

Catching prey is not easy and, 80 percent of the time, the quarry manages to get away. The hare, for example, adopts a zigzagging run to escape a wolverine. When pursued by a lion, an oryx will lower its horns, face the lion, and charge. And some fish will take on the color of the seabed to camouflage themselves.

For the penguins in the waters of Antarctica, life is much easier: when a shoal of fish arrives on their doorstep, they simply help themselves to a picnic!

On the other side of the world, life's not so easy for the Arctic fox. Often it has to make do with a few mouthfuls of seal stolen from a bear. So when it has the opportunity to catch a ptarmigan or a variable hare, it will devour it at one sitting. If prey are numerous—for example, when there's an abundance of lemmings—it sets up its own makeshift pantry: it buries several of these small rodents in the ice—as if it were a refrigerator—in the hopes it will find them again when food becomes scarce. Because the wolverine does the same with its prey, however, the Arctic fox will often uncover a wolverine's stores, and vice versa. So the smarter of the two will enjoy the best dinners!

When the shrike has caught too much prey, it stores the surplus by impaling it on long thorns or the spikes of barbed wire.

Tools

The orangutan uses its hand to scoop water into its mouth for drinking. This is one of the rare occasions it will venture into water, which it detests. When it rains, the orangutan uses a big leaf as an umbrella so it won't get wet.

Like the orangutan, all the great apes use tools, chiefly to obtain food. The chimpanzee breaks off a thin branch from a tree and carefully peels away the leaves. This it coats with saliva and pokes into a termite mound; insects stick to it, and the chimpanzee pulls it out and eats them. Leaves are very useful for drinking river water. The chimpanzee either uses one leaf like a spoon or chews up several together to make a compact ball that will act as a sponge; he soaks up water with it and then squeezes it out into his mouth.

But apes are not the only animals to use tools. The sea otter feeds mostly on shellfish. An expert at floating on its back, it uses its stomach as a kitchen table on which to break open shells with the aid of a pebble.

Birds are also inventive: the Egyptian vulture (a small, white variety) will take a stone in its beak and use it to crack open an ostrich egg. If the stone proves too small to break the shell, it chooses a bigger one and starts again. It will continue to try out stones until it finds one big enough to do the job. Similarly, when a crow's beak isn't strong enough to open an egg, it will throw it down onto a hard surface.

The song thrush uses a flat stone as an anvil on which to break the shells of snails.

Varying the Menu

Whatever the weather, the polar bear patrols the ice in search of food. Best of all, it hopes to find a hole in the ice where the seals come up for air. However, it will need a great deal of patience and cunning to catch one.

A predator's food depends on its habitat, the climate, the season and, of course, the number of available prey in its territory. A winter that's too cold and snowy, an extra-hot summer, or a fire or flood can all upset the ecological balance and thus put an animal's life in jeopardy.

The polar bear is omnivorous—it eats whatever it can find. So during the Arctic winter, it turns its attention from seals and varies its menu: its first choice is birds and their eggs, then it turns to lemmings and variable hares. For dessert, it will pluck a few leaves and berries. Unfortunately, in recent years polar bears have become increasingly inclined to visit both the numerous scientific bases on their territory and the scattered native settlements, where they scavenge the refuse.

Like the polar bear, the red fox also varies its diet by season. Although rabbits and small rodents make up the bulk of its food, its menu is extraordinarily varied. For instance, it takes advantage of the morning dew to gorge itself on earthworms and, in the autumn, frequents vineyards where it feasts on the ripened grapes. On the coast, it raids the nests of seabirds, swallowing their eggs and gobbling their chicks. Whatever the conditions, it always manages to find something.

With the arrival of snow, prey becomes scarce. The variable hare will now find it harder to escape the pursuit of a determined and hungry lynx.

The Rainy Season

After months of scorching heat resulting in a shortage of grass and, most important, water, zebras appreciate the arrival of the rains on the African savanna.

On the African savanna, the rainy season begins in November, though at first the storms produce only a few drops. The rain brings new life, but there's also the threat of fire. Because the grass is still dry after months of scorching heat, lightning starts numerous blazes. The animals must now flee these infernos, and old enmities are set aside: lions, antelopes, wild dogs, and warthogs can be seen fleeing side by side in their haste to avoid the flames. When the fire is over, life takes up where it left off, and once more each animal must find ways to avoid being eaten by its neighbors.

In February and March the heavy rains return. This is the time on the savanna when the trees and grass turn green again. The lakes and rivers overflow, and thousands of birds swoop down on the newly created marshes to gorge themselves on fish and succulent grasses.

The rainy season is also the time when zebras, gazelles, gnus, and other ruminants give birth. It's the most difficult period of all for the young, who are at the mercy of lions, cheetahs, and wild dogs with offspring of their own to feed. But Nature has arranged things well: there are plenty of young animals gambolling under the protective gaze of their parents, and it's only the weakest who will end up being eaten.

Sheltered by an acacia, a pair of hartebeest hesitate to venture out in the rain to feast on the long-awaited growth of new grass.

The Long March

Nothing can halt the migrating gnu: even the River Mara. In a huge cloud of dust, and accompanied by a few zebra and antelope, each year they relentlessly pursue the same paths across the savanna.

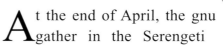

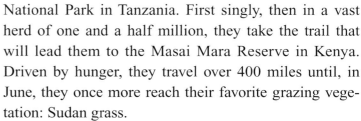

At the end of April, the gnu gather in the Serengeti National Park in Tanzania. First singly, then in a vast herd of one and a half million, they take the trail that will lead them to the Masai Mara Reserve in Kenya. Driven by hunger, they travel over 400 miles until, in June, they once more reach their favorite grazing vegetation: Sudan grass.

On this long journey, the gnu are accompanied by about 300,000 gazelles, 200,000 zebras, and 10,000 eland.

Year after year they take the same paths, forging trails across the African plain. This last big animal migration is especially dangerous. Of the young under one year of age, only one in ten will reach its destination. Several hundred adults will also die, from exhaustion and attacks by big cats, or from drowning in the River Mara, which awaits them at the end of their journey. Crossing this river is a nightmare. The gnu trample over each other, disappear into the muddy, turbulent waters, and—worst of all—are ambushed by armies of Nile crocodiles, who wreak havoc among the weakened animals.

At the end of October or beginning of November, the whole herd sets off on the return journey to the old grazing grounds.

The leopard makes the most of the gnus' long march. Lying in wait by river crossings, it pounces on the weakest animals.

In the Desert

The giraffe lives on the African savanna, where it feeds mainly on acacia leaves. It ventures only rarely into the semi-desert sub-Saharan zone because of the shortage of food and water there.

Deserts present extremely difficult living conditions, from the lack of water and intense heat of Africa's Sahara to the wind and cold of the Gobi Desert in Central Asia. To survive in such places, animals have had to adapt to the harsh environment.

The indefatigable addax (an antelope) ceaselessly treks the sands of the Sahara searching for the next tuft of grass. To protect itself from the sun's rays, its coat, gray in winter, turns completely white in summer. It can survive for several months without drinking, making do with moisture extracted from occasional grasses in the desert. Its stomach, however, has a reserve of several pints of water, which it can draw on as a last resort.

In the Gobi Desert, temperatures rise to 104 °F in summer, but drop to –22 °F in winter. All year round the wind blows at gale force. This is the habitat of the saiga antelope, an animal with a long, bulbous nose enabling it to filter the air it breathes, thus protecting its lungs from the bitter, snow-laden winds and burning dust storms. Its short, dense coat insulates it, summer and winter, from variations in temperature.

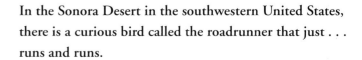

In the Sonora Desert in the southwestern United States, there is a curious bird called the roadrunner that just . . . runs and runs.

Cold and Snow

The female Japanese macaque gives birth to just one young at a time. At birth, the baby weighs a mere pound. It snuggles up against its parents for protection from the cold and snow.

An animals' natural environment can be hospitable or harsh. Climate (or temperature) is only one thing they have to adapt to; various other factors are involved as well.

In Japan, on the island of Honshu at an altitude of almost 5,000 feet, the temperature drops to –4 °F in winter. It's here, among other places, that the Japanese macaque lives. Its long, thick fur protects it from the cold and snow. It also takes advantage of the island's natural hot water springs, which are at a constant temperature of 100 to 140 °C. It enjoys invigorating baths and then dries itself off by lounging on the surrounding hot stones.

The Rocky Mountain goat lives in the high peaks of the west coast of the United States. This goat may be seen at an altitude of 13,000 feet, gambolling on rock faces with a 50-degree slope. To help it keep its grip, it has short, sturdy legs and hooves that are split in two, with a V-shaped opening at the front that acts like a pair of pincers. Their hooves are also pointed to provide anchorage, with rough, nonslip undersides. In winter, when the temperature plummets to –40 °F, this goat sleeps in the snow to protect itself from the cold! The snow insulates the animal by trapping body heat, maintaining an average body temperature of 20 °F.

The high peaks of the Himalayas are the realm of the snow leopard. In summer it will venture to a height of 19,500 feet in search of fresh food.

Birth in the Antarctic

It is springtime on South Georgia, and the young king penguins are molting. Their thick brown baby down is slowly replaced by the elegant black, white, orange, and gray-blue tunic of the adult bird.

The cold not only makes it hard to find food and keep warm, but also presents problems at breeding time; on the Antarctic ice, giving birth and raising young are undertakings fraught with peril.

The king penguin doesn't build a nest. Instead, the female lays a single egg, which she places on her feet. She protects it from the cold by draping her brood pouch (a special fold of skin near her stomach) over it. About every two weeks, the parents swap places. This changeover, however, is fraught with dangers. The egg is fragile, and it has to be kept at the same temperature throughout the incubation period: if it falls to the frozen ground, all is lost.

When the chick has hatched, the parents also take turns feeding it. Fed with fish and krill, it's soon big enough to join the rest of the penguins. At this stage of their development, all the chicks are gathered together in a huge group known as a nursery. This allows both parents to concentrate on feeding their offspring: the chick must eat as much food as possible because, two months after its birth, it will begin a winter lean period lasting five months! After this fast, the chick is fed by its parents until it molts. When it has acquired its adult plumage, shortly before its first birthday, it's able to hunt for itself in the sea.

The parents must also eat as much as they can before returning to land to molt. They often increase their body weight by as much as 20 pounds. A food reserve is vital: the molt consumes a lot of energy and the birds must molt regularly to renew their plumage and keep it waterproof and insulating.

Resembling a little leaping imp, the Rock-hopper penguin, with its punk haircut, is conspicuous on the Antarctic ice.

Why?

In spite of attempts to protect it in the wild, the giant panda's future is still very uncertain. Its low rate of reproduction and the destruction of its habitat are the main causes of its decline.

Humans do not seem to respect nature. Our exploitation of natural resources and our disregard for the environment are leading to disaster. The forest is the most dramatic example of this: every day another species is threatened with extinction as a result of deforestation—insects, flowers, birds, and all the great apes.

Every day, thousands of tons of pesticides are sprayed onto our planet. In France, for instance, the house martin population has dropped by more than 80 percent in less than ten years as a result of the disappearance of the insects these birds feed on and the destruction of their nests.

Every day, tons of plastic refuse and thousands of gallons of hydrocarbons are dumped into the sea. Turtles suffocate when they swallow plastic bags, having mistaken them for jellyfish; oil slicks devastate our beaches and bring death to seabirds.

Every day, human beings slaughter animals for no reason. For example, because the rhinoceros is now a protected species, traditional Asian pharmacy, which uses its horns in medicines, has to make do with the horns of the male saiga instead. Today, only one male remains for each hundred females, and the global population has diminished by 90 percent!

The Tasmanian wolf—the last great carnivorous marsupial—disappeared for ever at the beginning of the twentieth century.

How Can We Help?

Until recently, it was thought the koala was safe from extinction because its numbers appeared to be increasing. But disease has decimated its population. Add to this the destruction of its habitat and, once again, its future is uncertain.

Throughout the world there are National Parks, wildlife parks, and conservation areas. Associations dedicated to protecting wildlife are springing up all over the place. In animal reserves and the wild, there are programs to protect endangered species and reintroduce them to the wild. Without such programs, what would have happened to the koala, the nene goose, Père David's deer, the African elephant, or the Arabian oryx? Saving animals and their environment isn't, however, just a job for the experts; it's a responsibility we all share.

What can we—ordinary people—do on a day-to-day basis to preserve the environment and to protect existing species?

Perhaps, quite simply, we should learn to respect animals and the environment more. We should acknowledge, as Antoine de Saint-Exupéry put it, that the world does not belong to us—that we merely hold it in trust for future generations. This means realizing that every time an animal disappears, a little bit of ourselves is lost. It means being prepared, every day, to give up a few more of our creature comforts to conserve the world's natural resources—particularly water and timber. It means swapping our guns for cameras. It means laying aside our fear of the wild, the unknown, and the different.

One of the most touching success stories of recent years has been the reintroduction of a herd of Przewalski horses to the wild. These horses now run freely across the plains of Mongolia.

PHOTOGRAPH CREDITS